to W. D.

Elegy

Prepare:

Sw.	Celeste and Lieblich
Gt.	Small Diapason
Ch. or Solo	Viol, 8ft. Flute and Tremulant
Ped.	Gt. to Ped.

G. T. THALBEN-BALL

Lieblich only
rit.
a tempo
Gt. Diaps., with Sw. coupled
mf
pp
Gt. to Ped.

Gt.
Sw. (full)
Gt. to Ped. in
Gt.
Gt. to Ped.
cres. poco a poco

ff tutta forza
ff
Diaps.
dim.
rit.
f
f
Solo Viol and Tremulant
espressivo
poco rit.
p
Lieblich only
Sw. Celeste and Lieblich
a tempo
pp
Sw.
soft 32 ft